SHAKE UP YOUR LIFE

Jennifer Dall Ed.D
Shake Up Your Life/ Jennifer Dall Ed.D —1st ed.

Paperback ISBN: 79-8-9952108-1-8

SHAKE UP YOUR LIFE

30 Tiny Experiments to Shake Things Up When You Need Change

JENNIFER DALL, Ed.D.

CONTENTS

INTRODUCTION

I'M NO stranger to shaking things up. In fact, in the past few years I've done some of the biggest shake-ups of my life. I quit my full-time job to start my coaching practice, I started speaking at conferences and events, and I launched a publishing business. Those big shake-ups felt great. It helped move a lot of stuck, stale energy into a space that felt exciting and full of life.

However, when you are feeling that sense of staleness in your life, you can't always quit your job, move across the country, or start a whole-foods, plant-based travel company for vegans ala Rick Steves. (No really, I tried to do that once, but that's a story for another day.)

Recently, when I felt myself on the brink of a shake-up, I thought about what it would look like to make tinier, more subtle shake-ups, that still evoke the sense of newness and change. Subtle shifts that could bring about *change* and yet not further *disrupt*!

Enter: tiny experiments. I began playing with the idea of tiny experiments—small, low-consequence, yet fun ways to shake up my life to see what could come from it. For me, experiments are lighter than goals or projects, so they feel a bit more doable. I decided to try one to see what would happen; I was shocked at the results!

The first tiny experiment I chose was what I called, "Visit Your City as a Tourist" (check out page 26 if you want guidance on doing this, too). While exploring, I stumbled upon a very cute, small shopping village that I now love. I found a Sunday farmer's market with great tacos, a falafel to die for, a great coffee shop that is my new favorite meeting place, and adorable little specialty shops that I now frequent often. All walkable, all hidden away. I've even considered buying a house there for the vibe! (A future shake-up, maybe?)

I now do this particular tiny experiment multiple times a year, and I am astonished at how I am able to see the city I live in under a new light. I've found a small arts and crafts museum and even a little hidden dog park in a peaceful and relaxed area.

This first simple, tiny experiment taught me that I can shake things up in small, daily ways, if I choose to do so. There is always something new to explore, a new route to take, or a new connection to make.

I suppose the question now is...*where will you start?*

BEFORE WE BEGIN:
THINGS TO KNOW

Before we begin, here are some things you need to know.

Choose Your Timeframe

The tiny experiments in this book are broken down into several categories including Micro-Actions (30 minutes or less), Quiet Reflections (simpler, inner work), and Short-Term Shifts (within a week or two). Choose yours based on how much time or energy you have in your life now.

Make It A Challenge

What to take it even further? Consider turning these tiny experiments into a bigger challenge. Here are some ideas:

30-DAY CHALLENGE

A 30-day challenge is a sweet spot—long enough to see progress, short enough to feel doable. For 30 days, choose one small, daily experiment inspired by this book. Keep a simple log in a notebook or notes app. You can turn this into a mini-journal, a list, or a creative record. If you like accountability, invite a friend to do their own 30-day shake-up alongside you, and compare notes at the end.

	X	X	X	X	X	X
X	X	X	10	11	12	13
14	15	16	17	18	19	20
21	22	23	24	25	26	27
28	29	30				

If you want to really shake things up, make a custom punch card for your tiny experiments. Each time you complete one, punch your card. Choose a reward when your punch card is complete. For example, you can set up a punch card to have 10 tiny experiments. And the reward? A solo brunch date, a pastry from your favorite bakery, or a relaxing spa night. Once you punch all 10, you can treat yourself with something special. This is a fun, visual way to incentivize shaking up things in your life.

cut along the line here

Note

Each experiment comes with room on the page to take notes after the experiment is complete. This helps you reflect on the experiment and what you learned about yourself in the process. If you need or would like more room, feel free to use a separate notebook to detail all your tiny experiences. (Plus, who doesn't love a new journal?!)

Just Try It!

These are experiments. They may work for you now, or they might work later. If something seems scary (but not dangerous), perhaps that is a sign to try it!

HOW TO CHOOSE YOUR TINY EXPERIMENT

THIS BOOK contains 30 tiny experiments. Here are some ways you can use this book:

1. **Start at the Beginning**: Work your way through, page by page.

2. **Leave It Up to Chance**: Randomly flip to a page and complete the experiment found there.

3. **Skim and Pick**: Skim through the book and start with the experiment that speaks to you most.

4. **Choose Your Experiment Type:** The tiny experiments are broken down into several categories including Micro-Actions (30 minutes or less), Quiet Reflections (simpler, inner work), and Short-Term Shifts (within a week or two). Choose based on how much time or energy you have in your life now.

Tiny Experiment Steps

Once you choose your experiment, next you'll:

1. Read
2. Reflect
3. Research
4. Brainstorm
5. Schedule and commit
6. Reevaluate and do it again, if you like

Reflection Questions

It's important to reflect on your tiny experiment, as you can learn more about yourself. Here are some questions to reflect on after an experiment:

- What do I like or not like about this and is there a way to adjust or use it?
- What did I learn about myself?
- How can this experiment help me make a change in my life?
- Am I looking for a big change or small change and why? (Both have their purpose.)

MICRO-ACTIONS

LIFE IS busy and, sometimes, you don't have time to create a big, elaborate plan to shake things up in your life. Rather, you need a shift *right now*.

Micro-actions are small, low-effort experiments designed to change your energy in under 30 minutes (often, in even less). These are for the moments when you think, *"I need a change... right now."*

You might have five minutes. A lunch break. A pause while waiting in a pickup line. No prep, no overthinking—just open your notebook or notes app, step into the moment, and do one, small thing. Each micro-action is a simple activity meant to help you shake off stuck, heavy, or stale energy and to reconnect with yourself quickly.

Tiny actions can create real movement. Let these tiny ones shake things up now.

Pay It Forward

RIGHT NOW, pause and choose one small act of kindness that you can do in the next 5-15 minutes. Maybe you can hold a door for someone, send a genuine thank-you text, write a kind note, or pay for someone's coffee behind you in the drive-thru line. This does not need to be over the top or elaborately planned. Sometimes, the simplest kindness makes the biggest impact.

One of the best ways to shake off stale, old, or negative energy is by doing something kind for someone else. Kindness can break loops of frustration, doubt, and heaviness, because it pulls your attention outward and reminds you of what really matters. This tiny act isn't about fixing the world—it's about shifting your energy here and now, so you can show up every day a little happier.

REFLECTIONS

19

Say "Hi" Today

THINK ABOUT the times that getting a random message from someone made your day. What if you could do this for someone? The simple act of saying "hi" to a friend, or even a stranger, can give you a mental-health boost.

Browse through your contacts, past texts, or emails. Who have you not been in touch with that you could reach out to? Who would you like to hear from? Remember something about them and ask a question, if you can. Reach each out and say "hi." Or let them know something recently reminded you of them. Don't overthink it. Keep it light and easy. Have no expectations.

Be open to what new conversations, reconnecting, and reaching out could lead to in your life. A new friend, job, relationship? Idea for a change? You never know where a simple "hi" could lead.

REFLECTIONS

Style Yourself New

You know that feeling when you buy a new outfit or see someone wearing something that is totally different from your usual style? It's like a fresh new way of seeing yourself!

Instead of shopping at the mall or online, try shopping in your closet. Search for your favorite pieces, pair them with a different accessory (scarf, pin, overshirt, pants), and get a whole, new feel for free.

Or how about that item you loved at the store but haven't ever worn? Rescue it from your closet, grab a few other pieces, and play around with making it yours. You loved it for a reason when you bought it. Do you need to pair it with jeans instead of a skirt? Boots instead of flats? A complimentary color? Reconnecting old items in new ways can breathe life into your wardrobe without breaking the bank.

REFLECTIONS

Learn a New Game

THINK BACK to when playing games was just part of life. Board games at the kitchen table, and pickup soccer matches with friends. Now is your chance to learn a new game or pick up an old favorite—cards, virtual, or something physical.

Games invite playfulness back into your life. It's also a great time to socialize, meet new people, or deepen connections you already have. They get you moving, laughing, learning, and connecting.

Think of a game you've never played but always wanted to try—cards, a board game, a video game, or something physical like tennis or soccer. Or choose something brand new that's been popping up everywhere and sparking curiosity. (Pickleball, anyone?)

Take five minutes and put it into motion: search for a local community league, look up a game club, or text a friend and say, "Want to try this with me?"

It's not about being good or having fancy equipment, it's about your willingness to try something new. And who knows where that might lead you?

REFLECTIONS

Visit Your City as a Tourist

Look around your community and choose one place you've always been curious about—then go visit it. Search for places you've never heard of, places you *always* wanted to visit, and the silliest, touristy places that you would "never" go to. Maybe it's a museum, a park, a community space, or an unusual shop or restaurant you've driven past a hundred times but never stopped. Sometimes, the most meaningful discoveries are hiding in plain sight. I once stumbled upon a small, natural area tucked just off a busy road I'd traveled forever—and now it's my go-to spot when I need a quick reset in nature.

Shake off the mindset that exploration only happens when someone is visiting from out of town. Revisit favorite places you haven't been to in a while and seek out spots you've never heard of—even the cheesy, touristy places you'd normally skip. Go solo or bring a friend. Take photos, jot notes in a journal, or share what you find, so others can discover it, too.

Once you're out there, stay open. You might find a new favorite place, stumble into a volunteer or job opportunity, or run into someone you know. If you're looking to shake things up, start by asking: What's already in my backyard that could change my perspective? Sometimes a small adventure close to home is all it takes.

REFLECTIONS

Free-Day Challenge

WHO SAYS an experiment has to cost money? Discovering free events in your community can be part of your tiny experiment itself. It is the perfect invitation to explore spaces that already exist to bring people together. With a little research, your city or town will feel full of opportunities.

Some of my favorite spots to explore for free opportunities include local libraries, coffee shops, and community newspapers. Often, these spaces have additional community bulletin boards that advertise upcoming events and town happenings. Even cooking stores, art spaces, and bookstores might host things like free food demonstrations, author talks, or hands-on workshops. Local museums or gardens have free entry on certain days and offer other lectures, demonstrations, and DIY-style events that are open to the public.

To stretch yourself a little, challenge yourself to talk to one new person at each event. No pressure—even a quick "hello" or a short conversation counts. This is especially powerful if you're introverted or feel like meeting people doesn't come naturally. Because it's free, there's zero commitment—you can stay for five minutes or an hour.

REFLECTIONS

Tiny Adventure Walk

Only have a few minutes free between tasks or while waiting for someone? Go on a Tiny Adventure Walk. After all, adventures can happen anytime, anywhere. Bonus points if you go in a direction you don't usually go.

Open the door, step outside, and see what the world has to offer. Even a short walk brings fresh air, movement, and a mental reset. Let it be simple exercise or add a mindfulness layer—notice your breath, your footsteps, the light, the sounds, the small details you normally pass by.

You might also collect *pocket treasures* along the way. A smooth stone, an interesting leaf, a phrase overheard, a photo, a color combination, a moment that makes you pause. These tiny finds can become reminders that curiosity is always available.

Stay open to what you notice—a shop you want to return to, a community space you didn't know existed, a path worth exploring another day. This experiment can be repeated endlessly. Wherever you are, as long as it's safe, you can step outside and take a Tiny Adventure Walk.

REFLECTIONS

Reverse To-Do List (aka the To-Done List)

To-do lists can sometimes suck the fun out of everything. And yet... we still have things that need to get done. Here's a simple shift you can use anytime: a Reverse To-Do List.

On a day when you already know what needs to be done—maybe it's in your head, your calendar, or a notebook—don't write the list in advance. Instead, write things down *after* you complete them. Dishes done? Phone call made? Emails answered? Walk taken? Check. Check. Check. Check.

This small change helps your brain register success as it's happening. *"Look at all the things I finished"* feels very different from *"look at all the things I still have to do."* It builds momentum, confidence, and a real sense of accomplishment—even on ordinary days.

Want to take it further? Add a reverse-reward layer. Write down when you took a break, rested, laughed, or did something just for fun. Those count, too. This list isn't about pressure. Rather, it's about noticing that you are moving forward.

REFLECTIONS

Swap Your Sensory Style

Do you find yourself sleepwalking through your day? Shake things up by intentionally using all five senses! That's right—bring in your senses and add a new element to the expected.

We experience life through our senses, but, sometimes, we stop paying attention. This experiment invites all the senses back in and opens you up to new ideas and new ways of doing things. You might learn something that leads to a bigger change.

Try eating a snack with your eyes closed and notice the flavors, textures, and smells you usually miss when visuals take over. Listen to a song you've never heard or one you've heard a hundred times. Close your eyes and let the sound wash over you. Or pull up the lyrics and read them out loud like a poem, seeing the words clearly without the music guiding you. Walk barefoot—inside or outside—and notice the feeling under your feet, the sounds of your movement, and how those sensations travel up through your body.

What other small ways can you invite more sensory experiments into your day, even for just a few minutes? Pay attention to what you notice. This simple experiment can quietly change how present and alive you feel.

REFLECTIONS

What Surprised Me Today?

WHAT IF today's experiment happened without you even planning it? It's the end of the day and you wish you had taken the time to try a tiny experiment. Reframe your thinking and find success in a different way.

Instead of feeling bad, jot down the details of your day. Look for things that surprised you, things that you didn't really notice before. Where did you go, what did you see, who did you talk to? Not what you *expected* to see but what you *actually* saw.

Did someone say something kind to you? Did you eat or drink something different? Were you able to meet someone where they were in a different way?

Notice the tiny things throughout the day, and you might be surprised by it. Dig deeper and keep going. Consider making this a part of your nightly routine. Take the space and write down: *One Thing That Surprised Me Today...*

REFLECTIONS

QUIET REFLECTIONS

SOME CHANGES don't come from doing more. Instead, they come from slowing down and listening. Quiet reflections are intentional pauses that lead to change. These are gentle, unrushed moments where you step away from noise, input, and expectations to check in with yourself.

Think of this as a quiet date with yourself. A Saturday afternoon. A favorite journal. A warm drink. Your dog curled up nearby. The door closed, notifications off, and a clear *Do Not Disturb* sign—literal or symbolic. This is time to think, feel, notice patterns, and let insights surface without forcing them.

These reflections aren't about fixing or judging. They're about creating space for clarity. When you make space for quiet, meaningful change often follows naturally.

Travel Back in Time

People love time-travel movies for the thrill of going back and seeing past versions of the main character through today's eyes. When Marty McFly traveled back in time, he gained new insights into his parents and himself!

Step into your magical time-travel machine (a souped up DeLorean?) and imagine yourself as a child or teenager. Who were you? Did you like to play outside, dress up, or create adventures in your neighborhood? What were your interests and dreams? What were you good at?

For me, I remember the little girl who wanted to share her creativity by running a catering business, being an ambassador, and working at a radio station as a DJ!

Look for themes that repeat—creativity, learning, helping, movement, curiosity, being outdoors. Choose one theme and ask yourself: Where does this live in my life right now?

Would you like to invite it back in? Maybe in the same way or maybe in a completely new form that fits who you are today. This isn't about going backwards in time—it's about reclaiming parts of yourself that still matter.

REFLECTIONS

Tend to Your Social Garden

Imagine a beautiful garden. Flowers, butterflies, shrubs, a calming fountain, and a few weeds and dead plants. Where is your eye drawn? What would you change or nurture?

Your social life is like a garden. If it isn't tended to, you may lose track of what is in there and not notice something unwanted taking over. Researchers found that people you associate with influence your outlook and choices. Take an inventory of your social garden—is it filled with good friends, family members, and coworkers? Or people from the past who are no longer adding beauty to your life?

If you are in a new chapter of your life, look for others who will come along on your journey and bring support. Give yourself permission to take a break as someone may not be adding to *your* life *now*, but they once did and may later.

REFLECTIONS

43

Ask Before Your Act

REACH OUT to a few people you trust and ask them: *"If all bets were off, what out-of-the-ordinary thing could you see me doing? What is your dream for me?"* Send it as a text or email.

To make it fun, gamify it—offer a silly prize, coffee, or bragging rights if you choose their idea to try. You know when you get an email survey, and they offer 10% off or a free, fun thing if you respond? It's like that, and it also boosts engagement, motivation, and fun!

Pay attention not just to the answers but to how it feels to read them. What surprises you? What resonates? Surveys like this can be revealing—not just about what others see in you, but what they see as possible. That can be powerful fuel to shake things up in your life. You set the rules. What would you like to act on and why?

REFLECTIONS

45

Map Out Your Dream Life

GRAB A beverage of choice, find a quiet space, and put on your dream cap. A dream cap is like a thinking cap but about your dreams. If you could live any life, what would it be like? Where would you live, who would you be with, what would you do with your time and energy? What would be important to you?

Write it out, sketch it, or make it visual by cutting images from magazines or creating a digital collage. Take as much time as you need. When brainstorming, often the best ideas come AFTER the first ideas.

Now, look at your current life with an eye open to possibility. What's in it? How close are you to parts of this dream life? What area lights you up and is attainable now? Celebrate what you are doing to create your dream life. Then, choose one small experiment that could move you two steps closer. You may discover you're nearer than you thought.

REFLECTIONS

47

Dig Deep for What You Admire

THERE ARE so many inspirational people out there to learn from. Let's find out who inspires you and why!

Set a timer for 15 minutes and brainstorm people you admire—famous people, your next-door neighbor, your 4th-grade best friend, someone you read about in the news, or even a fictional character. Select one of these people and do a deep dive. Who are they and what have they done? More importantly, what is it that you admire about them? Is it that they started a charity to provide plants to kids in the city? Is it that they had a passion and followed it? Or is it something else?

Looking below the surface can help us figure out what we truly value and would like to add to our lives. Often what we admire most in others points directly to values we want to live out ourselves. Repeat this exercise with a few more people you admire and notice the patterns that emerge.

REFLECTIONS

49

Rediscover Your Positive Traits

WHEN PEOPLE give you praise, what do they say? What positive traits do people value in you?

Not sure where to start? Text your closest 5 friends or family members and ask them. Maybe they value your ability to make friends, be there in an emergency, or make the best dessert? Get curious and ask them to tell you more about why this is important. Notice what shows up again and again.

If this trait matters to you, how can you use it more intentionally? Could it become part of your work, your relationships, or even something you share with others? Some people turn their strengths into classes, videos, guides, or tiny "how-to" books. What comes naturally to you might be exactly what others are craving.

REFLECTIONS

Reflect on Your Change

WHEN YOU look for opportunities to make change, sometimes you don't give yourself credit for what you have already done.

Let's take a look at this. List five ways you've already made changes in the last year. You might even wish to organize this by areas of life—work, relationships, health, learning, or family—to see a more holistic overview. Compare where you were a year ago to where you are now—what you were hoping for versus what's happened?

Which changes do you want to continue? Which ones need adjustment? Writing these down turns vague growth into something you can actually build on.

REFLECTIONS

53

Brainstorm Your Future

Not sure what your future will bring? Let's have some fun brainstorming! Pick a random number between 6 and 60. (Or, if you want to gamify it, roll a set of dice.) The number you pick represents the number of months into the future you are looking. If you picked or rolled 7, that represents 7 months. If picked or rolled 23, that represents 23 months.

What would you like your life to look like personally, professionally, socially, physically, and/or creatively in that time frame? For each area, brainstorm five steps that could move you in that direction.

What would you like to be doing in your career?

What would you like to be doing in your social life?

What would you like to be doing physically?

What would you like to be doing creatively?

List five steps for each. Then, pick one area where you can simply take one step now. Do that. Then, plan out and put the other steps on your calendar. The future becomes far less overwhelming when it's broken down into intentional, doable actions.

REFLECTIONS

55

Do Over

REMEMBER IN school when something didn't work out and you yelled, "Do over!" You can apply the kindness of a reboot to your life at any time!

We've all had brilliant ideas that fell flat. At best it didn't work; at worst, it was embarrassing, expensive, or humiliating. Think of a project that didn't go as planned, yet you are still interested in it. Take an honest look at the project, your original reasons for wanting to do it, and why it didn't work. Then look at it through the eyes of you now—not the you who first tried it, but the you at this age, in this place, with what you know today. Is it salvageable? All of it? Parts of it? Could you approach it with more effort or less? A different end goal? A new mindset? Could involving other people make it more fun, supportive, or grounded?

What are three ways you can do it over today? Go for it again!

REFLECTIONS

Your Life as a Mixed Tape

Life in Seven Songs—a popular podcast of *The San Francisco Standard*—asks famous guests to tell their life in 7 songs. The host Sophie Bearman always has fascinating conversations, and the listeners get a glimpse into the lives and minds of all sorts of people.

Remember making mix-tapes for a friend, a crush, or a road trip? This gave a glimpse into a time and place in your life and mind. That's the power of music. At different times, your taste in music and what you need from music changes. You may have forgotten what was so important to you at 15, what got you through that rough patch at 22, or the song that always reminds you of that special occasion or special person. Yet, when you hear it now, you are transported back.

Pick 5-7 songs that represent your life now. Review them and write down the story of what they represent. Share it with a friend and invite others to choose 5-7 songs of their own. Come back and review that period of time in your life. Notice how things changed.

REFLECTIONS

SHORT-TERM SHIFTS

SOME CHANGES don't deliver an instant boost, but they do build momentum in your life that your future self will be happy about. Short-term shifts are small experiments that take a little planning, patience, or follow-through before the payoff shows up.

This section is about research, setup, and gentle commitment—signing up, reaching out, scheduling, gathering what you need, and letting anticipation do part of the work. You may not feel the reward immediately but each step signals that something new is in motion.

Think of these as bridges between intention and action. Not rushed, not overwhelming. Just enough structure to shake things up and create meaningful change in the near future.

Take a New Class and Learn a New Skill

WHAT HAVE you always wanted to try?

If you take a look around, you will see that there are opportunities to learn everywhere! Community centers, libraries, colleges, niche stores, gyms, and studios are just a few places that offer introductory, one-time, and short-term classes. Some are free and most are low-cost, so there isn't much of a financial or time barrier.

Research shows that learning keeps your mind active, introduces you to new ideas that may change your life and to people you didn't know before.

Brainstorm ideas you've always wanted learn more about. Belly dancing? French baking? Horseback riding? Rock climbing? Tai Chi? Dream big. Write down five ideas. Then write down five more.

Pick one or two of your ideas and do a little research. Is there a class starting soon? No? That's okay. Save the idea, move on to the next, and keep looking. Sometimes the first idea isn't the winner, but it leads you to the one that is.

Search broader terms like "cooking classes," "foreign language," or "community classes." New interests often hide inside general categories. Stay curious. The goal isn't to commit forever—it's to experiment and learn something new about yourself.

REFLECTIONS

Teach a Class

DID YOU ever consider that YOU may be the expert or inspiration that someone else is looking for? What is your secret skill? Photography? Yoga? Vegan cooking? Organization?

Think about what people often come to you for help with or advice on. Make a list of all the things people ask you about. Pick one you'd enjoy sharing and plan to teach a class about it.

To get started on your first class, ask yourself these questions:

- *How will I share this class?* Video, online, podcast, small book, in person?
- *What will I be sharing?* What is the specific skill or takeaway?
- *Where will it be held and when?* Online, a community space, your home, someone else's?
- *Who will I invite?* List 5–10 people you could tell, contact each, and say,
- *"I'm trying something new—would you share this with three people and support me?"*

You don't need to be a complete expert. You just need to be willing to start.

REFLECTIONS

Volunteer

"JUST VOLUNTEER somewhere!" is often tossed out as an answer when we are looking for new adventures, but this isn't always as easy as it sounds. How do you know where to go or what to choose? Let's look at some places to start your search. Do you enjoy working with animals? How about kids? Your local animal shelter or school may be just what you need. Does a community theater need ushers or a museum need docents? Perhaps an annual event or weekly farmer's market could provide flexible opportunities?

When signing up to volunteer, consider trying something outside your usual skill set that you don't often get to use. This can help you learn and polish new skills. Additionally, research shows that volunteering boosts your health, expands your social circle, increases sense of purpose, and exposes you to new experiences and perspectives, all while making a positive impact on your community. Volunteering is a win-win because helping others quietly often helps you understand yourself even better.

REFLECTIONS

Do It Solo

PLAN A solo vacation doing something you've always wanted to do. Close your eyes and imagine someone hands you a free pass to take a trip. The rules? It has to be somewhere new, doing something you've never done before.

Rock climbing? Glamping? Visiting every gluten-free restaurant in a city? Taking a long-distance train trip? If your vacation dreams are bigger than your budget, get creative. Scale it down. Shorten the time and bring it closer to home. This isn't about how far you travel or how much money you spend; it's about creating a unique experience for yourself.

Traveling alone can boost your self-esteem, allow you to experience new things on your own timeline, and open you up to a world of possibilities. Plus, you can bring your experience home and share all the things you did and learned with others.

REFLECTIONS

Do One Thing Your 8-Year-Old Self Wanted

RESEARCH ON "inner child" work shows reconnecting with early interests can increase creativity, self-compassion, and joy. It's not about being childish, it's about feeding all parts of yourself.

Think back—what did 8-year-old you want to be? If you can't remember, ask your family members. Then brainstorm 10 ways you could do something related to that goal today. Then brainstorm 10 more. Choose one and find unique ways to put a plan into action and do it!

For example, if you wanted to be a firefighter, then maybe you could take an emergency preparedness class, visit a local fire station open house, learn about community needs during fire season, or make a donation. Get creative and take one action.

REFLECTIONS

Try 5

Here's a short-term shift that can help you break out of a rut and look for new treasures. Commit to visiting five new restaurants or coffee shops. It's easy to get stuck in the same routine—the place down the street, the usual Friday night order, or the place that is on the way home from work. To get out of a rut, try something new! Pick up a local guidebook or search online for visitor favorites, dietary-specific lists, or new ethnic cuisines you've been wanting to try. You may discover your new favorite place that you'll frequent instead of always grabbing pizza down the street every Friday. As a bonus, you'll support local establishments and possibly make some new friends.

Small changes in routine can refresh how you experience your everyday life. Keep a record here in the note pages in the back of this book of where you went and about your findings. This can be added to at any time.

REFLECTIONS

Confirm Your Friend Dates

Make one friend date a week for three months. Saying, "We should get together sometime," is easy. Following through is the hard part. Let's make this an experiment.

Three months is only 12 dates. One a piece of paper, make a list of 1–12 (or even 1–15). Start listing names from your contacts and jot down something you could do with each person—coffee, a walk, a movie, a dog park visit, a new or favorite restaurant, a book signing, or a volunteer event. Note any schedule limitations.

Then start inviting. "Hi, Sarah! I found a new coffee place downtown and realized we haven't talked in ages. Would you be free next week? Friday morning works for me." Be open to different times or ideas and move on gracefully, if it's not the right moment.

REFLECTIONS

Try One New Activity (for Three Months)

Commit to one new class, talk, or event each week for three months. As we grow up and become adults, we often stop learning or taking classes—especially when just for fun. Classes are powerful experiments—they help you discover what you like, what you don't, and, sometimes, what you want to change.

Look into community centers, colleges, museums, local bulletin boards, and even stores. Want to learn to write a book, watercolor, start a garden, make fresh pasta, learn a language for a country you've always wanted to visit, take photos, or refresh your high school Spanish? Commit to a series and focus on the skill and the community that comes with it.

REFLECTIONS

Revisit a Past Goal

WHAT WAS the last exciting goal you made? Or the one before that? Write these goal(s) down as you remember them—whether you achieved them or not. Now, let's take another look at them with a growth mindset. A "growth mindset," coined by Carol Dweck, a psychologist at Stanford University, is the idea that a person's capacities and talents are not fixed and can be improved over time.

Now, let's revisit your goal(s) with a growth mindset. Set aside perfection and aim for growth. For example, was your goal to have *no sugar for a month*? This sets you up to win or lose. What if the goal, instead, is *to be mindful of the sugar you eat*? This sets you up for growth.

Revisiting a past goal with the lens of a growth mindset encourages exploration, curiosity, and fun. Where might this take you?

REFLECTIONS

Make a New Friend in a New Group

IT'S EASY to get looped into friends in your age group, as you often cluster by life stage—school, kids, career. These friendships are great, and you can feel great connection with those whose current situation is similar to yours. However, think about friendships you've had outside those parameters. What did you value about that friendship? Maybe they offered perspective, wisdom, or playfulness? Friends from a diverse pool bring different points of view, passions, and experiences.

Brainstorm five places in your life where you already interact or could interact with people outside your typical group. These could be places you are already a part of or, maybe, stretch yourself and try a different class with people you haven't interacted with before. Take a tiny step and introduce yourself to new folks. Be curious. Ask questions. You can learn from anyone, if you remain open.

REFLECTIONS

Host an Event

SOME OF us may cringe at the thought of hosting an event but take a deep breath and remember that it doesn't have to be the party of the decade!

Start by committing to hosting one social event—coffee and cookies, a walk, or a potluck. What sounds like fun? It doesn't have to be big or expensive. Consider selecting a theme if that feels better, such as bringing your favorite book, album, or movie. Encourage people to bring one new friend.

If hosting feels intimidating, start tiny with just two people, for one hour; go out in the world with a shared purpose. Or try something where you share responsibility. Maybe it's a small group and each friend takes a turn hosting. Stay open to letting others join over time. These small events and tiny changes can create big shifts down the line.

REFLECTIONS

Start a Silent Club

WHAT IF you could get together with other people *and* do your own thing? A silent club can have a purpose like reading, writing, or crafting, or can be BYOA—Bring Your Own Activity.

A silent club builds on a concept of "body doubling" in the neurodivergent community. Body doubling is similar to "parallel play" for little kids. Essentially you are in the same space, soaking up companionship, all while doing your own thing. Your brain believes it is time to focus, and you get the added benefits of companionship.

How to start? Pick a date, ask people to invite one friend, and advertise in your community. Consider partnering with a coffee shop or bookstore; many are happy to provide space. It's a win-win—they get exposure and community presence, you get a place to read, write, and connect. No local space? Try an online meeting and invite people from anywhere.

Start with introductions and a short check in of what each person is working on. Set a timer for an hour or two and *start*. Five to ten minutes before finishing, allow everyone to report back on something they did or learned.

REFLECTIONS

YOU DID IT!

WHETHER YOU tried one, four, or all 30 tiny experiments, you started down a new path to shake things up in your life. But the fun doesn't have to stop here. You can enjoy picking up this tiny book at any time and selecting a different experiment (or redoing one you've already tried).

Thank you for joining me in this shake-up adventure! I always love hearing your stories and successes, so if you would like to share, please don't hesitate to reach out and find me on www.adhdholistically.com. You can email me from there, sign up for one of my newsletters, and see what else I'm up to.

Speaking of sharing, do you have a friend who would love this book? If so, please share it! Maybe you could come up with new tiny experiments to try or even start your own tiny experiment club. You never know what you might just learn about yourself and others! It starts with just one tiny experiment.

ACKNOWLEDGEMENTS

I want to thank those who helped provide the space to take part in this Tiny Book and publishing experiment!

To Jackie, I watch you shake up your life as you grow and am so proud!

To Janice and Traci, two of my biggest supporters who understand the urge to shake things up, a little bit at a time.

To Lindsey and Alex, two brilliant, creative women who have helped me so much on this publishing journey.

ABOUT THE AUTHOR

Dr. Jennifer Dall is an advocate for women with ADHD+1. She is an author-publisher, coach-consultant, speaker, and lifelong educator. As the founder of ADHD Holistically LLC and Curveball Press, her mission is to help women navigate life's curveballs and create a life that finally feels like theirs. She holds degrees in education and counseling and an Ed.D. in educational psychology, and is a certified yoga teacher and trained grief educator. She lives in Southern California.